YOUR KNOWLEDGE HAS VALUE

Bibliographic information published by the German National Library:

The German National Library lists this publication in the National Bibliography; detailed bibliographic data are available on the Internet at http://dnb.dnb.de .

Imprint:

Copyright © 2015 GRIN Verlag, Open Publishing GmbH
Print and binding: Books on Demand GmbH, Norderstedt Germany
ISBN: 9783668481084

This book at GRIN:

http://www.grin.com/en/e-book/370339/impact-of-company-income-tax-on-revenue-generation-of-federal-inland-revenue

Mivayi Japhet

Impact Of Company Income Tax On Revenue Generation Of Federal Inland Revenue Service (Msto) Yola, Adamawa State Nigeria

GRIN Publishing

GRIN - Your knowledge has value

Since its foundation in 1998, GRIN has specialized in publishing academic texts by students, college teachers and other academics as e-book and printed book. The website www.grin.com is an ideal platform for presenting term papers, final papers, scientific essays, dissertations and specialist books.

Visit us on the internet:

http://www.grin.com/

http://www.facebook.com/grincom

http://www.twitter.com/grin_com

TITLE PAGE

IMPACT OF COMPANY INCOME TAX ON REVENUE GENERATION OF FEDERAL INLAND REVENUE SERVICE (MSTO) YOLA, ADAMAWA STATE NIGERIA

BY

MIVAYI JAPHET

SBT/ACCY/ND/15/046

A PROJECT SUBMITTED TO THE DEPARTMENT OF ACCOUNTING, FACULTY OF ARTS, SOCIAL AND MANAGEMENT SCIENCES, IN PARTIAL FULFILMENT OF THE REQUIREMENTS FOR THE AWARD OF NATIONAL DIPLOMA IN ACCOUNTING, FEDERAL POLYTECHNIC MUBI, YOLA CAMPUS, ADAMAWA STATE

FEBRUARY, 2017

ACKNOWLEDGMENT

All appreciation is given to God almighty, the source of my study who saw me through my study, may his name be gloried. (Amen)

Also my warn gratitude goes to my supervisor Dr. Peter Teru for his support of putting me through even though it was not easy for him to guide me through the part of this success. May God Bless you.

I appreciate God for the life of my lecturers especially, Mr. Abel Tarfa, Mr. Benson, Mrs. Joyce, Mal. Bakari Maude, and many more for the role they play in impacting into me knowledge. My prayer is that they will never remain the same. My appreciation goes to Uncle Danladi Kotohulla for his prayer and financial support towards my academic programme.

I will not forget people that gave me this life, my parents in question who stood the ground of taking me to school even when I proof not to love the idea, but they patiently love and show me way on how to catch the fish myself. Mummy Elnah, I am reaping the benefit of your handwork, remain bless, also my daddy Japhet Maude for his financial support towards my academic programme.

Finally, I will like to thank special brothers, sisters and friends for their advice, My Mummy Omega Joshua, Bro Ibrahim Japhet, Godiya Japhet, Esther Japhet, Dorcas Japhet (kakas), Hyelda Joshua, Helen Joshua, Benjamin Joshua, Paul Joshua, the families of Samuel pella, Nyakwi Saidu, Madam Yemisi, Hapsat and All my course mate for their advice and prayers towards this success. May God Bless you all and grant long life and prosperity.

DEDICATION

This project is dedicated to Almighty God and to my parents Mrs. Elnah Japhet, Mr. Japhet Maude, My Siblings and Mrs. Omega Joshua.

TABLE OF CONTENTS

ABSTRACT

The increasing cost of running government coupled with dwindle revenue has led various state government in Nigeria with formulating strategies to improve their revenue. This project the impact of company income tax on revenue generation in Nigeria. The method used in collecting data for this research work is through primary, personal observation and secondary data as the major source of information. The researcher administered the questionnaires randomly to the staff of Federal Inland Revenue Services, registered Company Income Tax agents and in some public places in Adamawa State. One hundred (100) questionnaires were generally administered to all the various respondents at the rate of one questionnaire per individual. The data collected were analyzed using simple percentage. The analysis revealed that there is no any marked difference in the various respondents' general perception of Company Income Tax on government revenue generation and its impacts on living condition of people in Adamawa State. Therefore, based on the findings, the study recommends among others that; the government agency responsible for the collection of companies income tax, the Federal Inland Revenue Service (FIRS) should work in liaison with the Commission (CAC) to ensure that all companies registered in Nigeria i.e. Foreign and Domestic meet their tax obligations to the nation.

CHAPTER ONE

INTRODUCTION

1.1   Background to the Study

The increasing cost of running government coupled with dwindle revenue has led various state government in Nigeria with formulating strategies to improve the revenue base more so, the near collapse of the national economy has create serious financial stress for all tier of government. Despite the numerous source of revenue available to the various tier of government as specified in the Nigeria 1999 constitution, since the 1970s till now, over 80% of the annual revenue of the three tiers of government came from petroleum. However, the serious decline in the price of oil in recent years has led to a decrease in the funds available for distribution to the states. The need for state and the local government to generate adequate revenue from internal sources has therefore, become a matter of extreme urgency and importance. This need underscores the eagerness on the part of states. The need for state and local government to generate adequate revenue from internal sources has become aggressive and innovative in the mode of collecting revenue from existing sources.

Development is a sine qua non for modern civilization in order to carry out development at all nooks and crannies of the society, it is responsibility of the Adamawa state government to provide direct development to people to a certain level. Development is associated with funds and much revenue is needed to plan, execute and maintain infrastructures at the state level. The need revenue generated for such developmental projects, like construction of accessible roads, building in public schools, health care centres, construction of bridges are generated from taxes, royalties, haulages fines, and grants from the states, national and international governments. These funds could either be obtained internally or externally. Thus, the Adamawa state government cannot embark, execute and possibly carryout the maintenance of these projects without adequate revenue generation.

1.2   Statement of the Problem

Company income tax is one of the taxes that are imposed by government in Nigeria. There are various views for and against the imposition of company income tax in the opinion of (Omolehinwa 1990). Companies' income tax contributes insignificantly to the government general revenue profiles and therefore should be abolished.

In line with the above the Research observed that the disclosure of chargeable/taxable profit of companies are not honest with consequently leads to lower tax derivable from this sources.

More to this, where disclosure is made, separate accounts are prepared by companies in order to avoid paying the correct tax this is as a result of Nigerians corrupt tendencies i.e. tax evasion and or avoidance.

It is against this back drop that the researcher felt the need to critically examine these mitigating factors in the tax system in Nigeria in relation to the contribution of companies' income tax to the general revenue profile of government.

Therefore, this project is aimed at examining the growing trend in the assessment and contribution of company income tax on government revenue.

1.3   Objectives of the Study

The main objective of this study is to assess the impact of company income tax on government revenue generation in Nigeria. Specific objectives include the following:

i.   To determine the proportion of companies income tax contribution in relation to total government revenue.

ii.   To ascertain whether or not it should be abolished in view of the attendant problem in its assessment.

iii.   To suggest measures on how to improve the contribution of companies income tax to government revenue base.

iv.   To review the administration of the companies income tax and recommend improvement in its structure.

1.4   Research Questions

The following research questions were formulated to guide the study;

i.   What is the proportion of companies' income tax to total government's revenue?

ii.   What are the problems associated with assessing companies' income tax?

iii.   What are the measures to be taken to improve the contribution of companies' income tax to government's revenue base?

iv.   What measure should be taken with a view to reviewing the administration of the companies' income tax structure?

1.5   Research Hypothesis

The research hypotheses stated will be tested in two ways; the null hypothesis and alternative hypothesis.

Hypothesis one:

H_0: Company Income Tax has no significant impact on revenue   generation of Adamawa State

H_1: There is no significant difference between Company Income Tax and   sales tax in the volume of revenue generation in Adamawa State

Hypothesis two:

H_0: There is no significant relationship between Company Income Tax   and the living condition of the people in local government particular   Adamawa State

1.6 Significance of the Study

This study is basically concerned with the impact of companies' income tax on government revenue. The study will attempt to find the significance of this tax as a source of government revenue. Other taxes will be compared to companies' income tax so as to ascertain the difference between them.

The major tax which benefit from company income tax are petroleum profit tax, custom and excise duties and value added tax (VAT), have been chosen as yardstick to measure companies' income tax contribution since these are major taxes.

Due to the fact that value added tax was not introduced until 1993, its data is in complete and will therefore not be useful for regression analysis. Other taxes are not included are minor tax due to unavailability of data to show their contribution to government revenue.

1.7 Scope of the Study

The scope for this research study is for ten years (from 2003-2013). It should be noted that the area supported to cover are all the geographical zone in the country as the topic implies the contribution of the Companies Income Tax (CITA) to Revenue generation in Nigeria.

1.8 Definition of Key Terms

The following key words and variables will be given definition as they were used in this study, they includes:

Tax: - Refers to a compulsory payment of money or occasionally of goods and services from private individuals, institutions or groups to the government, it may be levied upon wealth or income or a surcharge on price.

Government Revenue: - This refers to all monies accruing to government which increase the funds over which the treasury has control without a comparable increase in debt obligation.

Income Tax: - An income is a levy on the financial income of personnel or corporation or other legal entities.

Company: - Is a form of organizing a business with a legal personality distinct from the individual taking part in it.

MSTO:-

Corporate Tax: - Refers to a direct tax levied by various jurisdictions on the profit made by companies or associations which often includes the capital gain of a company.

CHAPTER TWO

LITERATURE REVIEW

2.1 Introduction

This section reviews related literatures on the topic under study specifically; it examines the concepts of Company income tax, taxation, functions of tax system, major types of Nigerian taxes, determination of profits of Petroleum Company and taxation system in Nigeria.

2.2 Historical Background of Adamawa State

Adamawa State was created out of the former Gongola State in 1991, during the Gen. Sani Abacha regime. The splitting of Gongola into two came about the emergence of Taraba State and Adamawa State.

The State has large land mass of 42,158 square kilometer 1a1ng within Latitude 7°, 28°N and 10⁰, 8N longitude 11⁰. 30° 75⁰E and 13, 75⁰E. The 2006 census gave the population of the state as 3,024,851 with a density of 12 persons per square kilometers. (Adebayo, 1999).

Adamawa was call the Land of Sunshine because of the early rise of the sun before the day break and its late setting and it is also known as Land of Beauty because of the natural found among the people and in the environment. It is also known as the Land of the hidden treasure because of the abundant resources found in it. With a diverse ethnic and cultural group living in peace and harmony. (Adebayo, 1999).

The ethnic groups found in Adamawa State are: Margi, higgi, Chamba, Yandang, Bachama, Kilba, Gaanda, Fali, Yongur, Vere, Lala, Fulani among others. These ethnic groups live in segmented large and small communities speaking different languages and dialects with Hausa and English as the official Language spoken.

The majority of Adamawa indigenes are predominantly farmers, fishermen, businessmen and civil servants. The state is a very rich agrarian region where cash crop such as: beans, bambaranuts, groundnuts etc. are produced in a large quantity, while food crop cultivated includes, maize, rice, guinea corn, millet etc. Apart from cultivation, they involve themselves in animal rearing such as cows are in a commercial quantity.

Adamawa State shares boundaries with Cameroon in the East, Taraba State in the South, Gombe State in the West and Borno State in the North. Administratively, it is made up of 21 local government namely: Mubi North, Mubi South, Yola North, Yola South, Madagali, Michika, Maiha, Gombi, Hong, Song, Girel, Fufore, Demsa, Guyuk. Shelleng. Numan, Lamorde, Jada, Mayo Belwa, Toungo and Ganye Local Government Areas with Yola North as the state capital In terms of religion, Islam and Christianity are the math religion practice in the state.

2.3   Company Income Tax; An Overview

Companies income taxation deals mostly with the profit or gains of Limited Liability Companies, there are business organizations that are incorporated under the Companies and Allied Matters Decree (CAMD) 1990 usually, liability of member of this types of business/organizations are limited to only the capital that such members have contributed to the business.

Philipson (1946) stated that, the companies income tax in the colonial era, grew at a very slow rate due to the limited numbers of Limited Liability Companies, and moreover, most of these companies were owned and controlled by foreign nationals and profits were repatriated.

Anyaduba (1999) also stated that, Company Income Tax began in Nigeria in 1999, but was known then as Companies Income Tax Ordinance (CITO) not too long after, it was replaced due to certain anomalies that were discovered in its provisions.

In 1940, the Companies Income Tax Ordinance (CITO) was replaced by Nigeria Income Tax Ordinance (NITO) No. 4 of 1940. This new tax brought both individuals and companies under the same umbrella for the first time ever. This tax lasted until 1943 before it was replaced with Nigeria Income Tax Ordinance (NITO) No. 29 of 1943, under this view ordinance, tax rate was fixed at 50 percent.

However, if a company can prove that it had paid dividends out of its chargeable profits it will be relieved of some sums. The amendment continued over the even up to 1963 in 1961 Companies Income Tax Acts (CITA) remained the main tax legislation dealing with the assessment and taxation of companies throughout the country until 1979, when it was re-enacted as the Companies Income Tax Act (CITA) 1979 which was consolidated with the numerous amendments in to the Companies Income Tax Act of today. For a tax structure to be effective it must be efficient and apply equally.

2.4 Concept of Taxation

Taxation can be defined as a compulsory levy imposed on a subject or upon his property by the government having authority over him or his property (Akaule 1991) stated that the main purpose of taxation is to raise funds to meet government's expenditure. To him taxation should be regarded as a potential weapon of economic regulation. Anyaduba (1999) further adds that, taxation can also be defined as the process of or system of raising revenue through the levying of different types of taxes.

Taxation according to Ola (1985) is the demand made by the government of a country for compulsory payment of money by the citizens of the country. Various taxes have been put in place by governments in order to mobilize resources to finance public expenditure, which is a major function of any government especially in a developing country like Nigeria. No matter its political ideology the process of any government depends on its ability to generate sufficient revenue to finance an expanding non-revenue generating public service.

According to Akaule (1991) taxation is the raising of funds to meet governments expenditure, to him it is a potential weapon of economic regulation. Since it affects the amount that is available for spending by the private sector.

Aiyedun, (1996) also share the same view with Akaule, since according to him government uses taxation to promote economic and social policies.

If according to Aiyedun, (1996) taxation can be used to promote economic and social policies and Akaule (1991) stated that it is a potential weapon of economic regulation since it affects the amount available for private, sector spending effective taxation can then actually be one of the keys to Nigeria's economic development.

2.5   Functions of a Tax System

The objectives of a tax system which has long been reduced to three will be discussed:

i.   **Revenue Raising:** As stated by some economic scholars, taxes are raised to meet government expenditure and this is the key function of a good tax administration. In the absence of tax, the ability of the Federal government to meet its obligations to its citizens might be highly impaired. Indeed, it is sometimes suggested that without the largeness from the Federal government certain state of the federation might find it difficult to survive. Basic non-revenue yielding social amenities such as education, health, security defense, law and order cannot be ordinarily be provided by the free market. A review of the revenue of the Federal government shows that taxes has contributed immensely to the meeting of the expenditure of governments. By the way taxes are administered in Nigeria, it is evident that what is basically on the mind of the tax administrators in Nigeria is to raise revenue. That also appears to be the uppermost thing in the mind of a typical tax administrator, they even sometimes forget its impact on investment in the economy thereby mortgaging the chances of increasing the wealth of the nation on the long run, since some provisions in the tax law is disadvantageous to tax payers but increases revenue collection.

ii.   **Redistribution of Wealth:** This objectives is based on two premises: one, that taxation should basically rest on the ability to pay, thus, requiring that the greatest burden be borne by the rich. Therefore, taxes should have a built-in redistribution function. With reference to Nigeria, tax reverse is what is obtained since the rich who are supposed to represent the "fattest back" shun payment of taxes in any and every possible way. Thus, some writers have argued that this is due to the inability of Nigeria's tax authorities to deal strictly with this group of people.

iii.   **Management of The Economy:** Taxation as a Fiscal policy has helped also in the management of the economy, examples are the various tax reforms since 1995 which were supposed to release more money to the hands of the household, thus, positively affecting the economy.

2.6   Company Income Tax: The Economic Impact

Company income tax is a tax which mostly affect income especially in a developing country. On the grounds of efficiency and equity, company income tax has been subjected to criticism, some proposed its abolition others felt that states rather than the Federal government should administer this tax. The companies income tax in as much as the government embarks on it has to have additional source of revenue generation, and should be administered with caution since it affects the desire and ability of people to invest.

In the United States where Nigeria draws substantial inputs on tax matters, the effect of the tax on companies income tax drives between the before tax and after tax rates of returns on investment. For example an investment which earns as 20 percent before tax returns yields a smaller after tax returns to the investor. The others is paid in taxes; because of this tax bite, some investments that would have been attractive are not undertaken. Despite this however, there is no solid evidence that the overall level of the United States investments have been discouraged because of the existence of tax.

In addition to its possible effects on the level of investment in the economy, companies income tax has other economic efficacy or resource allocation consequences. There is therefore, the need to tax this companies in order to generate revenue from them, which could be used to provide the basic infrastructural facilities so as to encourage private investors, in general, the taxation potential of a country depends on some factors which be responsible for the yields gotten from taxes. Some of these are:

i.   The level of per capital income.

ii.   The degree of in equality in the distribution of that income.

iii.   The administrative competence/honesty and integrity of the tax gathering branches of government.

iv.   The social, political and institutional setting and the relative power of different groups (e.g. landlords and opposed to manufacturers Trade unions, village or community and organizations.

v.   Industrial structure of the economy and the importance of foreign trade, the significance of the modern sector, the extent of foreign participation in private enterprise, the decree to which the agricultural sector in commercialized as opposed to subsistence oriented agriculture.

Companies income tax is a tax on both domestic and foreign owned companies. In most developing countries this tax amounts to less than 2 percent of the Gross Domestic Product (GDP) compared with more than 6 percent in most developed countries. The reason why this tax raises so little revenue in most developing countries is that there is relatively less corporate activity in the overall economy as is the case in Nigeria, all attention is on petroleum profit tax since the oil sector is regarded as the most important sector in the economy not minding its detriment on the environment.

In the case of multi-nationals foreign enterprises, the ability of government in developing countries to collect revenue from them in form of taxes is often frustrated. Since these enterprises are able to shift their profit to partner companies in other countries offering the lowest level of taxation by transfer pricing.

Therefore by means of transferring price, multi-national companies are able to shift their profit from one place to another in order to lower their overall tax assessment while leaving their total profit unchanged. The concept of taxation should therefore not only be limited to monitoring the activities of companies, but what is even more important is the efficiency and integrity of the tax these laws. As observed by Professor Kaldor two ago, in most under-developed countries the low revenue yield of taxation can only be attributed to the fact that the tax provisions are not property enforced, either on account of the inability of the administrator to cope with them, or on account of straight forward corruption. Since no system of tax laws however, carefully conceived is protected against collusion between the tax administrators and the tax payers, an efficient administration consisting of persons of light integrity is usually the most important requirement for obtaining maximum revenue and exploiting fully the taxation potential of a country.

Although taxation is not the sole source of government revenue it is nonetheless an important avenue by which government finances its needs. Taxation does not guarantee that a tax payer receives a definite of direct protection from government for payment of tax but the benefits goes to anyone irrespective of the amount of tax paid. A collection of various taxes imposed by the state constitutes the relevant 5% tax structure of such state or that Nation. Therefore, tax reformers strive always to design and administer tax structures to fit in to the overall economic philosophy of the nation.

In Nigeria when put together the broad economic objective include:

i.   Price and exchange stability
ii.   Job creation
iii.   Sustainable growth

These have to be achieved through other ways such as sustained fiscal discipline and improved revenue generation. Any tax structure, that however yields maximum revenue from tax payers without concern for how such funds are put to use is bound to experience high level of evasion and avoidance.

In fact it would be best it policy makers should always be guided by the wisdom that if the public sector cannot make use of the funds which it extracts from private pockets, it should not levy such on them.

Looking at the companies income tax, and the percentage it contributes to total government revenue from 5.0% in 2009 to 6.1% in 2010 and 2011, and how from 2012 it began to decline from 4.8% to 4.2% and 4.5% respectively, it is obvious, that this decrease will have an adverse effect on the total revenue of the government. Apart from tax evasion, corruption among tax administrators, there are other factors that might be responsible for a decline in this tax which therefore makes government in an attempt to increase its tax base imposes levies such as minimum tax, withholding tax, which the private sector believe is unfair on them. What government could therefore do to improve this tax is to economically empower consumers so that the companies that are operating below capacity due to weak consumer demand would correct themselves as this will eradicate the persistent problem of weak and deteriorating infrastructures. In China, in a bid to increase its tax revenue base, government decided to impose a withholding tax on banks in China who depend on their overseas branches for finance/loans. Most of them were not happy about the decision, since domestic banks were exempted from the levy. Some analysis broadly sees the policy as made solely to punish foreign bank branches in Singapore and Hong-Kong. This therefore brought about a petition signed by foreign bank operators and forwarded to the Vice Premier in charge of the economy, objecting to the withholding tax. If this withholding tax has been causing concern for those to pay it in other countries of the world, the question is why will the government of Nigeria in the 2012 budget introduce an increase in the rate of withholding tax on all aspects of building construction and related activities and all types of contracts other than sale and purchase of goods and property?

The new withholding tax rate, which was introduced, was 5% (five percent). A withholding tax is a payment of tax in advance for companies whose turnover is fully subjected to deduction of withholding tax. The private sector and scholars sees the new rate as being on the high side punitive and also a disincentive to economic activities, especially where government does not make a refund of excess of the taxes that has already been deducted as source over the tax payable, worse still is that this excess can also not be carried forward or set off in a subsequent assessment years, therefore, the new withholding tax rate of 5% appears ill-advised according to (Omolehunwa 2012).

2.7 Major Types of Nigerian Taxes

Petroleum Profit Tax (PPT) petroleum profit tax deals with assessment of profit gotten from any petroleum trade operations or products. This includes oil obtained either by drilling or extraction in Nigeria. This tax is applied on only the types of companies in the petroleum industry which are:

i.   Crude oil producing companies.

ii.   The petroleum products marketing companies.

iii. The servicing companies which provide services tom oil producing companies. Examples of these services are drilling, interpretation of data that are gotten from oil fields etc.

Dada P.A. (2012) defines it as a tax on the profits of companies engaged in oil drilling business in Nigeria. The administration of the tax rest with the Federal Board of Inland Revenue a government agency on taxes.

2.7.1 Company Income Tax

Company income tax is the tax on the profits made by a company except petroleum companies. This tax is administered by the Federal Board of Inland Revenue (FBIRA); the tax deals with Limited Liability Companies. These are organizations or businesses that are incorporated under the Companies Allied Matters Decree (CAMD).

2.7.2 Personal Income Tax

The Personal Income Tax Decree (PITD) No. 104 of 1993, this Decree identifies taxable persons, it is a tax on individuals income. This tax is a form of revenue to the state collected by the states internal revenue service administrators. This tax is for residents administrators. This tax is for residents of states except the Federal Capital Territory, the Police, Armed Forces, Foreign Affairs Officers and nonresidents who pay theirs to the Federal Inland Revenue Service (FIRS). Civilians in the Police and

Military formation pay to their state of residence. Dada P.A. (1995) defines it as a tax, which is levied on an individual.

2.7.3   Capital Transfer Tax

This tax is about the most unpopular tax laws in Nigeria. The enabling law, Capital Transfer Tax Act of 1979, seeks to impose tax where a property is transferred to any person during the life of the person transferring the or upon his death. The reason why this tax is unpopular is because of its imposition on the properties of a deceased person, an act which is believed to be a taboo in certain parts of the country. This tax was abolished in 1995.

2.7.4   Capital Gain Tax

Capital gain tax can be referred to as tax on gains acquiring from increases in the market value of assets to a person who does not habitually offer them for sale and in whose hands they do not constitute stock in trade. The gain might be "realized" gains where the assets appreciate in value while still in the hands of the owners. Assets, which usually give rise to capital gains, include plant and machinery, land and buildings, goodwill etc.

2.7.5   Education Tax

(Education Tax Decree No. 7 of 1993). This tax decree No. 7 of 1993 is gotten from the FIRS. The tax imposes tax at a rate of 2 percent on the accessible profits of all incorporated bodies. This tax is applicable to all companies registered in Nigeria; the major aim of this tax is to gather sufficient funds for the maintenance on the nation's tertiary educational institutions. This tax is administered by the Federal Inland Revenue Service (FIRS) which pays all monies collected from this tax to the education tax board of trustees, established under the same Decree.

2.7.6   Value Added Tax

It is tax on goods and services (VAT) is a consumption tax which is eventually borne by the final consumer but collected is usually at each stage of production and distribution. This tax is backed by VAT Decree No. 102 of 1993, which came into operation on 1st December, 1993. This tax was imposed as a replacement for sales tax. VAT according to Naiyeju, J.K. (1996) was introduced to Nigeria due to the widening of the wealth/poverty gap. This lead to the government's exploitation of a means of redistributing resources as a way of improving the welfare of its citizens. This happening motivated the birth of the tax such as VAT in Nigeria. VAT is a tax that is less prone to evasion due to its nature, it is presently at a flat rate of 5% (five percent). A vatable person is therefore, one who trades in vatable goods and services. Goods and services exempted from VAT as stated by Alade, S.O. (1994) are goods such as medical, pharmaceutical products, basic food items, books and educational materials, newspapers and magazines, baby products, commercial vehicles equipment, and veterinary medicine products.

According to trade S.O. (1994) services exempted from VAT including medical services rendered by community banks and mortgage institutions and all plays and performances conducted by all educational institutions.

2.7.7 Taxation System in Nigeria; A Review

Tax system in Nigeria is tripartite and involves: -

i.   Tax policy

ii.   The tax laws and

iii. The tax administration

Tax administration in Nigeria is divided into three to take care of the three tiers of government, namely: the Federal, State and Local governments. The tax authorities of these three tiers of government derive their creation from Federal laws and they include:

i.   The Federal Tax Authority

Federal Board of Internal Revenue (FBIR) (section 1, 2 & 3 of CITA LFN (1990).

ii.   The State Tax Authority

State Board of Internal Revenue (SBIR) (section 85 A, B, +C of Personal Income Tax).

iii. The Local Government Tax Authority

Local Government Revenue Committee section 85 D, 8 E of Personal Income Tax Decree as amended by Decree No. 31, 1996.

Extracted from Inland Revenue Services.

CHAPTER THREE
RESEACRH METHODOLOGY

3.1 Introduction

Company Income Tax as clearly stated in chapter two of this research work is a tax in place of sale tax. It is an instrument of economic management in the hand of government for the generation of public funds especially in the local government system. Its introduction has a significant role and effectiveness on the economy development of the local government system. Therefore, this research tries to access such impact of company income tax system in Adamawa State.

In this chapter, we shall look at how the research is carried out. The emphasis will be on the method used for data collection, population of the study as well as the method used for the analysis of data obtained.

3.2 Research Design

Sankaratos S. (2005) defined research design as the basic plan which guides the data and analysis phases of the research project. The method used in collecting data for this research work is through primary, personal observation and secondary data as the major source of information.

3.3 Population of the Study

The target population for this research work comprise male and female from 18 years and above who are registered Company Income Tax agents, consumers and staff of the Inland Revenue Service (IRS) in Adamawa State.

3.4 Sample Size and Sampling Techniques

The sample consists of registered Company Income Tax agents, Inland Revenue Service staff and consumers in Adamawa State.

There are two basic techniques of selecting samples from population; these are probability and non probability selecting techniques. In this research, quota sampling which is a type of non probability sampling technique is used because it ensures that a certain number of sample units appear in the sample so that all these features are fairly represented.

3.5 Sources of Data Collection

The researcher administered the questionnaires randomly to the staff of Federal Inland Revenue Services, registered Company Income Tax agents and in some public places in Adamawa State. One hundred (100) questionnaires were generally administered to all the various respondents at the rate of one questionnaire per individual. After some few days, the researcher went back to collect the questionnaires from the respondents.

3.6 Instrument for Data Collection

a. Questionnaire: questionnaire which is a means by which a researcher get information through asking questions in a written form were distributed through personal visit and they were to fill in the necessary information in few days due time constraint they would have been given enough time to complete the questionnaire at their leisure. Copies of the questionnaire were issued to staff of the Federal Inland Revenue Service and registered Company Income Tax agents in the state.

The questionnaire comprises of structural and unstructured sets of questions which are divided into section "A" Respondents personal information, "B" for the registered Company Income Tax agents and "C" for Inland Revenue staff. Section A and B consists of ten questions each. The researcher also has discussion section with some consumers to know their view on the impact an effectiveness of Company Income Tax on their living condition.

b. Secondary source of data: Secondary data is obtained from existing written materials like textbooks, financial statement of some governmental parastatal as well as seminars papers that are essential to this research work were used. Personal observation was made over the years of Company Income Tax introduction to local government system was also relied upon.

3.7 Method of Data Analysis

The data collected were analyzed using simple percentage in this form:

Number of respondents that ticked Yes or No

Total number of Respondents

$$\frac{R}{N} = \frac{100}{1}$$

Where R = Total number of respondents

N = Number of Respondents who say Yes or No

CHAPTER FOUR
DATA PRESENTATION AND ANALYSIS
4.1 Introduction
In this chapter, the result of the information collected through questionnaire and interviews conducted in the study in relation to the central theme of this research project, the perception of the public on the impact of Company Income Tax on local government system is been presented and analyzed

Here we are concerned with Company Income Tax administrator, Company Income Tax registered agents and the general public on how they view Company Income Tax on government revenue generation in Nigeria bearing in mind its impact on their general well being.

4.2 Data Presentation and Analysis
In this study, the research pursued three (3) objectives. This section analyze, the data collected with respect to these objectives. However, the respondents characteristics is first analyzed with a view to understanding the respondent background and how this may affect their responses.

Table 4.1: Number of respondents

Respondent	Number	Percentage
Company Income Tax officers	25	25%
Registered agents	30	30%
Consumers	45	45%
Total	100	100%

Source: Field survey, 2015

A total of hundred questionnaires were distributed to Company Income Tax officers, registered agents and consumers. Out of this total 25 were given to Company Income Tax officers, 30 were given to registered Company Income Tax agents and 40 to consumers. The number represent 25%, 30% and 45% respectively.

Table 4.2: Responses on whether Company Income Tax has generated more revenue than the former sales tax

Responses	Number	Percentage
High	16	64%

17

Indifferent	6	24%
Low	3	12%
Total	25	100%

Source: Field survey, 2015

The table above shows that the entire Company Income Tax officers sample agreed that Company Income Tax has actually generated more revenue than the former sales tax. This means that the whole 100% had affirmative answer to the question. This is contrary to our assumption that Company Income Tax has no significant differences from sales tax in terms of revenue generation to Adamawa State.

Table 4.3: Company Income Tax officer's responses on the degree   of Company Income Tax evasion

Responses	Number	Percentage
High	16	64%
Indifferent	6	24%
Low	3	12%
Total	25	100%

Source: Field survey, 2015

From the table above, degree of evasion was the main response of Company Income Tax officers. Here a total of 16 officers represent 64% considered the degree of evasion to be high. Six of them representing 24% were indifferent while only 12% considered the degree of evasion to be low.

Table 4.4: Response of officers on company income tax rate charged   in Adamawa State

Responses	Number	Percentage
High	0	0%
Adequate	18	72%
Low	7	28%
Total	25	100%

Source: Field survey, 2015

The above table shows that 18 of the Company Income Tax officers sampled represent 72% accepted that Company Income Tax charged in Adamawa State is

18

adequate considering the present economic situation in the local government. While none of them agreed that the rate is high, 28% considered it to be low.

Table 4.5: Responses on preference between Company Income Tax and **sales tax**

Responses	Number	Percentage
Company income tax	26	86.67%
Sales tax	4	13.33%
Total	30	100%

Source: Field survey, 2015

The above table shows that 26 of the sampled Company Income Tax registered agents preferred Company Income Tax to the former sales tax. This represents the majority – about 86.67%, while only 13.33% preferred sales tax to Company Income Tax.

Table 4.6: Responses on Company Income Tax Evasion

Responses	Number	Percentage
YES	25	83.33%
NO	5	16.67%
TOTAL	30	100%

Source: Field survey, 2015.

From table 4.6 above, twenty five of the thirty of Company Income Tax registered agents represents 83.33% would evade Company Income Tax if there is an opportunity for them to do so. However, a total of five represent 16.67% would not evade Company Income Tax. These responses tallies with the Company Income Tax officer's responses on the degree of Company Income Tax evasion as shown by table 3 where 64% of the Company Income Tax officers considered the degree of Company Income Tax evasion as high.

Table 4.7: Responses on whether Company Income Tax is a major determinant of the high rate of inflation in Adamawa State.

Responses	Number	Percentage
SA + A	27	60%
Undecided	7	15.56%

SD + D	11	24.44%
Total	45	100%

Source: Field survey, 2015

From the table above, the perception of Company Income Tax registered agents on the relationship between Company Income Tax and the high rate of inflation in Adamawa State area appears mixed. Out of the total sample; the sum of those who strongly agree (SA) that Company Income Tax is a major determinant of the high rate of inflation were 27 representing 60%, seven respondents represents 15.56% were undecided, while 24.44% representing sum of those who strongly agree and disagree (SD) with the statement.

Table 4.8: Response on who is more affected by Company Income Tax

Responses	Number	Percentage
Producers	6	13.33%
Consumers	39	86.67%
Total	45	100%

Source: Field survey, 2015

The table above shows that out of the consumer's sample, 6 of them representing 13.33% consider the producers to be more affected by Company Income Tax through decrease sales while 86.67% considered the consumers to be more affected through increase in expenditure.

Table 4.9: Responses on Company Income Tax rate charged

Responses	Number	Percentage
High	5	16.67%
Adequate	24	80%
Low	1	3.33%
Total	30	100%

Source: Field Survey, 2015

Table 4.9 above shows that 3.33% of the sampled Company Income Tax registered agents indicates that Company Income Tax rate charged is low while 16.67% considered it to be high. The majority however, representing 80% considered the rate to be adequate. This falls in line with the Company Income Tax officers' responses on Company Income Tax rate charged in table 4.4 where 72% majority considered the rate charged to be adequate.

4.3 Findings and Discussion

Based on the interview administered to some segment of consumers about their perception of the impact of company income tax on government revenue generation in Nigeria, the following are the questions and general responses of various people who were the literate part of the population. This goes to show that as far as literacy rate is concerned of Which Adamawa State has a high illiteracy rate, therefore, majority of the general population were not aware of the company income tax system in Adamawa State.

It should be noted here that even those who were aware of the Company Income Tax operations in Adamawa State do not really know what it stood for. Therefore they feel that it is simply a strategy by the government to further squeeze life out of the people to increase it own revenue.

It was also found out from the interview that majority of the consumers do not actually make their purchases where Company Income Tax is being charged. Due to the unorganized market structures in Adamawa State, registered Company Income Tax agents where very few and they are only those that deal with large stocks. Thus, for the general consumers who buy mainly from small retail shops, they only pay their Company Income Tax in form of increase prices without actually knowing. This is why majority of the people did not know whether Company Income Tax exists or not.

The result of the interview also shows that majority of the consumers while agreeing that Company Income Tax has caused price to go up or increase did not agree that Company Income Tax is the major determinant of the rate of inflation in Adamawa State and local government system in general, this conclusion tally with the stand of the registered agents. They felt that Company Income Tax rate was adequate and its effects on price was not enough to be the main cause of the hyper – inflation which Adamawa State and local government system in general is facing. In summation, they viewed Company Income Tax as having negative effects, but not the majority determinant, of the falling standard of living.

On the question of their impression about Company Income Tax as a mean of revenue generation, some of the consumers viewed it from two perspectives. Firstly, they felt that if government intension was only to enhance the rate of revenue generation, increased taxes from people income is not the right channel. On the other hand, if the aim of Company Income Tax was overcome the deficiencies of the sales tax system, and then Company Income Tax should be used as a means of revenue generation.

The general conclusion of the consumers was that since the Company Income Tax rate charged was not too high and government was generating substantial amount from it, Company Income Tax could serve as a good instrument of revenue generation to Adamawa State. The consumers were however apt to warn that the issue of using Company Income Tax as a means of revenue generation might be pushed too far and its repercussion on the condition of living would better be imagined than real.

The result from the data collected did not shows any marked differences in the various respondents general perception of Company Income Tax as a means of revenue generation and its effects on prices and living condition of people in Adamawa State.

The responses of Company Income Tax officers, consumers and registered agents on their preference between Company Income Tax and sales tax showed a strong preference for Company Income Tax over sales tax. The Company Income Tax officers perceived Company Income Tax as having a boarder base, generate greater revenue and proved to be less difficult in administration. The registered agent's strong preference for Company Income Tax to sales tax was due to the ease of the transfer of the incidence of Company Income Tax to consumers.

The Company Income Tax rate charged in local government system that is the flat rate of five percent was viewed by majority of Company Income Tax officers and registered agents as adequate. Given the prevailing economic condition of the local government system, the 5% was viewed adequate to raise substantial revenue for the government.

On the grounds of equity, the uniform rate system falls short of the principle of equity in taxation. Thus, the burden of Company Income Tax tends to be more on the marginalized masses who spend a large proportion of their income on consumption. However, since Company Income Tax in local government system ad valorem, that is, levied on commodities according to their value, the burden does not fall so heavily on the poor.

As gathered from the data, Company Income Tax has been achieving its goal of revenue generation well enough on this question; the Company Income Tax officers gave a 10% affirmative answer. They unanimously agreed that Company Income Tax is generating substantial revenue and even much more than what was generated by sale tax. Consumers however expressed their lack of confidence in the local government in spending the revenue generated from Company Income Tax.

On the issue of Company Income Tax's effects on prices, the consumers as well as registered agents all agreed that Company Income Tax has led to rise in prices. The Company Income Tax officers attributed only a five percent increase in the cost of product to Company Income Tax. Thus a marginal rise of price in consonance with the 5% tax, unfortunately the rate of price in most cases was high as 5%. This was attributed to the exploitative tendencies of the sellers and not to Company Income Tax. It is important to note this point, that the increase in price brought about as a result of the 5% Company Income Tax rate is not sufficient enough to be a major determinant of inflation. 27 registered agents that is 60% were of the opinion that Company Income Tax was not a major determinant of inflation.

Although price rise with the 5% rate of Company Income Tax , when the various agents opined that the consumers were the most affected, consumers themselves do not hold Company Income Tax as the cause of their increased cost of living.

CHAPTER FIVE

SUMMARY, CONCLUSION AND RECOMMENDATIONS

5.1   Summary

The thrust of this study was to establish whether or not the company income tax contribution to government's revenue is significant. In doing this, the proportion of company income tax in relation to others and the total government's revenue was put into consideration. The study was guided by the H_0 hypothesis; which stated that there is no impact of company income tax on government's revenue and the alternative H_1 which stated that company income tax has a significant impact on government's revenue.

In the review of related literatures, the view of various scholars were sampled, while the study is premised on the theory propounded by the classical economist Adam Smith which posits, that any tax regime should be guided by the principles of equity, certainty, convenience and administrative efficiency.

The study leaned greatly on the secondary source for the sourcing of data used. This was particularly advantageous because the information used have undergone; editing verification and testing. The econometrics statistical model of specification and multiple regression was used in the analysis of data obtained for the study. The data covered government's total revenue from the company income tax, petroleum profit tax, and non-oil revenue over a period of 12 years, that is from 1997-2008. The findings of the study indicated that no single tax source is large enough to meet government's revenue needs.

There is also the indication that the company income tax which is the focus of this study contributes the least to government's revenue and its contribution is almost insignificant when compared to other revenue sources.

5.2   Conclusion

The main objective of this study is to establish the significance of the company income tax to government revenue; the result of the analysis of the data obtained for the study led to the conclusion that company income tax's contribution to government's revenue in Nigeria is insignificant. This situation can however be blamed on a lot of factors, most obvious of which is the insincerity and lackadaisical attitude of tax administrators, to the collection of government taxes. Another related issue is the advantage taken by foreign and domestic companies of the porousness in the administration of the tax to evade it.

5.3   Recommendations

Though it is the view of some scholars like Omolehinwa (1995), that the companies income tax should be abolished, this study will however like to differ from this opinion, and make the following recommendations on ways of improving the revenue from companies income tax;

1.   The government agency responsible for the collection of companies income tax, the Federal Inland Revenue Service (FIRS) should work in liaison with the Commission (CAC) to ensure that all companies registered in Nigeria Foreign and Domestic meet their tax obligations to the nation.

2.   All loopholes exploited by companies especially foreign ones to evade the payment of tax, such as profit transfer to subsidiaries, in other countries should be blocked.

3.   Tax administrators should wake-up to their responsibility with regards to the collection of the tax.

4.   The government should work harder at attracting foreign investors.

5.4   Suggestion for further Study

It has been proved once again through recent data that the company income tax's contribution to national revenue is still very low when compared to other sources; this has made the government to concentrate only on sources that are doing relatively well. This study is suggesting that another study can be made which measure the impact, the absence of company income tax may have on government's spending capacity if it is abolished as is being suggested in certain quarters.

BIOGRAPHY

Adebayo A. (1969) Nigeria Federal Finance: Its Development, Problems and prospects and prospects. London Hutchinson Educational.

Adewale, S. (2010) "VAT Hike as Deuth Knell on Economy" Daily Sun. June 21st.

Aiyedun, E. A. (1996);   Principles of Economics. Published in Nigeria.

Alice B.A, (2002) Nigerian Tax Prudence. Akure: Elsic Publishers

Anyaduba, J. O. (1990);   Company Income taxation in Nigeria" United City Press, 1999.

Bolaji B. (1994) "Miracle of Value – Added Tax". Daily times December 2nd.

Bolaji B. (1995) "Challenges of an Effective Value – Added Tax" Daily Times February 12th.

Dandago K.I and Alabede I.O, (2006) Taxation and Tax Administration in Nigeria; Kano Triumph Publishing Company Limited.

Dowling, E. I. (1992);   Introduction to Mathematical Economics; Schaums outline series. McGraw.

George E.L et al (1973) "The value – added Tax in Developing countries" Journal of international Monetary fund vol. 20, No.2.

Glenn P.J 91991) Tax reform: Lesson learned in Reforming Economic   system   in developing countries. Harvard: HiiD, Harvard   University.

Ibrahim B. (1995) "The VAT Renaissance" Daily champion. January 16th.

Kaldor N. (1995) Will underdeveloped countries learn to tax in Reading on taxation in developing countries. The John Hopkins University

Kontsyiannis (1991);"Theory of Econometrics". Elbs Macmillan Education Limited.

Lipsey, R. G (1983); "An Introduction to Positive Economics; English language book society/Welderfed and Nicolson.

Musgrave R.A and Musgrave P.B, (1989) Public finance in theory and   practice. 5th edition. New York: McGraw Hill Book Company.

Naijeju, J. K. (1996);"Value-Added Tax the facts of a positive tax in Nigeria. Kupand Public Affairs.

Naiyeju J.k, (1996). Value Added Tax (VAT), The facts of a positive tax in Nigeria, Lagos: Kupag Public Affairs.

Nigerian Tax News Vol. 1, No. 2 December 1995.

Ojo Seyi, (1998) Element of Tax Management and practice in Nigeria. Lagos: Sagibra Tax publications.

Omolehinwa, (1985);   Paper presentation topic: The role of Company Income Tax sector in the Development of Nigeria tax system.

ParkiIdisi and Barth Oshionebo (1998); Practical Guide to thesis and project work. Kinds and Queens Systems Limited.

Report on First Nigeria Economics Submit (1993); Spectrum books Limited. Second Annual Conference of Chief Executives of Nigerian Public Enterprise Theme: Productive Management in Nigerian Public Enterprise May 12th – 13th 1983.

Richard, Milka (1992); Improvising Tax Administration in developing Countries, IMF.

Department of Accounting

Federal Polytechnic Mubi, Yola Campus

Adamawa State

P.M.B 25, Mubi

April, 2017

Dear Respondent,

RESEARCH QUESTIONNAIRE

I am a student of the above named institution, undertaking a research on " Impact of company income tax on revenue generation of federal inland revenue services(MSTO) Nigeria: A case study of Adamawa State" in partial fulfillment of the requirement for the award of National Diploma in Accounting. Data is however needed to facilitate the study.

Therefore, I wish to solicit your cooperation in the supply of data by completing the attached questionnaire.

Be assured that all the information supplied will be treated confidentially and used only for academic purpose.

Thank you,

Yours Faithfully,

MIVAYI JAPHET

SBT/ACCY/ND/15/046

APPENDIX II

QUESTIONNAIRE

SECTION A

BIO – DATA:

1. What is your occupation? ....

2. Sex: Male [ ]   Female [ ]

3. Marital status: Single [ ] Married [ ] Divorce [ ] Widowed [ ]

4. Age: 18 – 24 [ ] 25 – 30 [ ] 31 – 35 [ ] 36 – 40 [ ] 41 and above [ ]

5. Educational Qualification

      (a) SSCE [ ] (b) Diploma [ ] (c) HND [ ] (d) Degree [ ]

      (e) Others specify ....

SECTION B

Question 1 – 10. STRICTLY TO COMPANY INCOME TAX REGISTERED AGENTS.

1.   Do you support the use of Company Income Tax as a source of revenue generation?

      Yes [ ]   No [ ]

2.   Do you think that Company Income Tax is charged on all goods and services?

Yes [ ]   No [ ]

3.   Do you remit Company Income Tax collected as soon as it is due?

Yes [ ]   No [ ]

4.   Has Company Income Tax increased the prices of your goods?

Yes [ ]   No [ ]

5.   Do costumers complain about prices?

Yes [ ]   No [ ]

6.   Who in your opinion is more affected?

Producers [ ] Consumers [ ]

7.   Do you consider Company Income Tax rate(s) charge as low

Low [ ] Adequate [ ] High [ ]

8.   Would you support an increase on Company Income Tax rate?

Yes [ ]   No [ ]

9.   What do you think are the problems of Company Income Tax as a means of revenue   generation?

_____

_____

10.   What would you suggest should be done to improve on company income tax administration?

_____

_____

SECTION C

QUESTION 11 – 20 STRICTLY TO STAFF OF INLAND REVENUE

11.   Do registered agents remit payments willingly?

Yes [ ] No [ ]

12.   Do you use force sometimes before they pay?

Yes [ ] No [ ]

13.   Are all goods and services taxed equally?

Yes [ ] No [ ]

14.   Do you consider Company Income Tax rate(s) charge to be:

Low [ ] Adequate [ ] High [ ]

15.   When compared to the former tax, does Company Income Tax yield much higher revenue?

Yes [ ] No [ ]

16.   Are their clients who default / evade payments?

Yes [ ] No [ ]

17.   If question 16 is yes, what is the degree of default or evasion?

Very high [ ] High [ ] Indifferent [ ] Low [ ] very Low [ ]

18.   Are Company Income Tax able person / organization requiring to advice the Company Income Tax directorate on charge of status?

Yes [ ] No [ ]

19.   Is there any way to increase the number of Company Income Tax able person / organization?

Yes [ ] No [ ]

20.   Do you think Company Income Tax has a great effect in the local government system economy?

Yes [ ] No [ ]

INTERVIEW QUESTIONS TO CONSUMERS

1.   What is your name and occupation?

2.   Do you have any knowledge about value - added tax in local government system?

3.   Have you ever been ask to pay Company Income Tax in your purchases?

4.   What do you think about the statement that Company Income Tax is a major determinant of the present high rate of inflation in the local government?

5.   What are the general effects of Company Income Tax on living condition of the people?

YOUR KNOWLEDGE HAS VALUE